IMPRESSIONS OF YEMEN

In memory of Madeleine Dumage

IMPRESSIONS OF YEMEN

Pascal and Maria Maréchaux

Flammarion
Paris - New York

Locations featured in the book

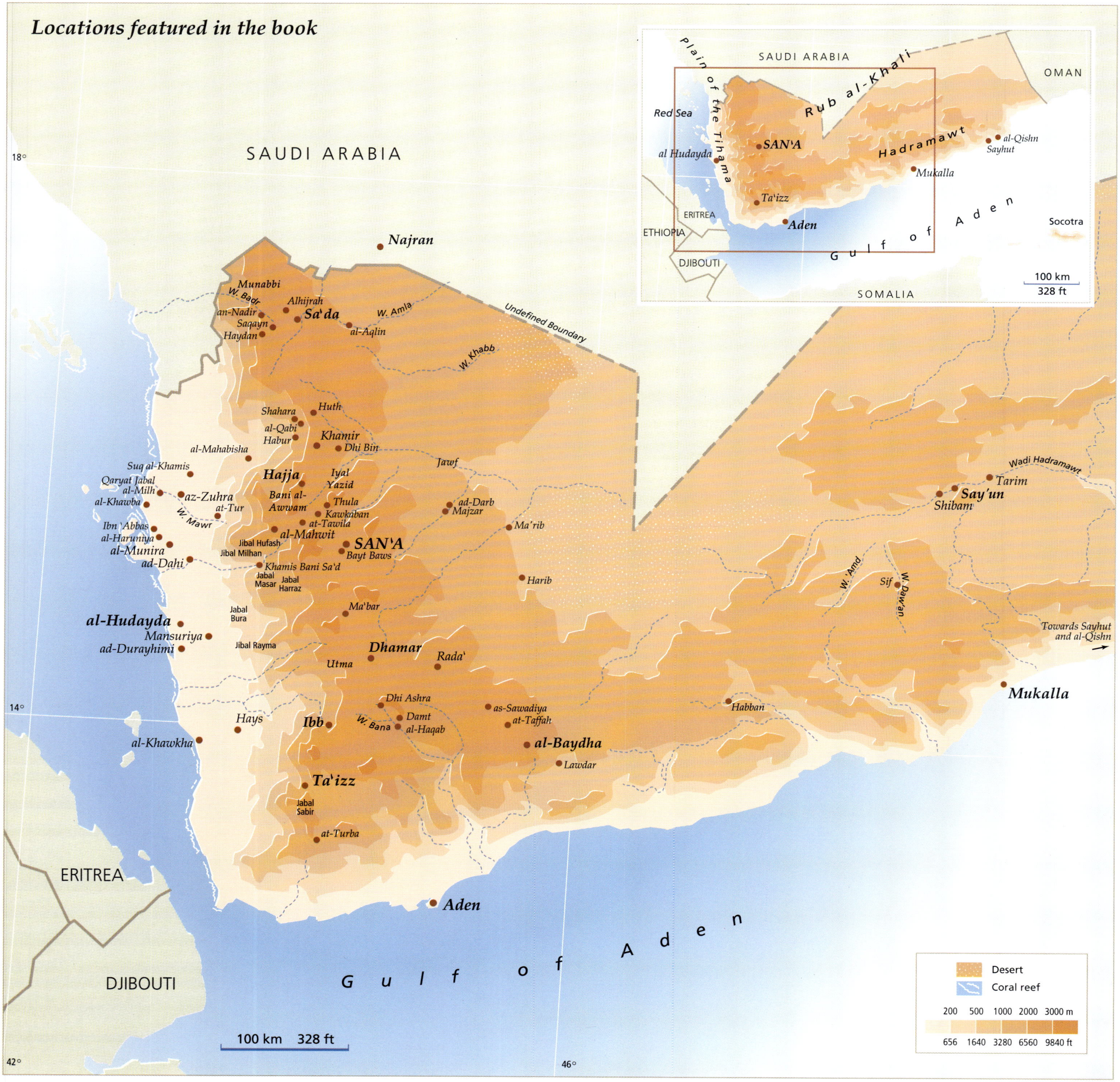
SAUDI ARABIA
OMAN
Plain of the Tihama
Red Sea
Rub al-Khali
SAN'A
al Hudayda
Hadramawt
al-Qishn
Sayhut
Mukalla
Ta'izz
ERITREA
ETHIOPIA
Aden
Socotra
Gulf of Aden
DJIBOUTI
SOMALIA
100 km
328 ft
18°
SAUDI ARABIA
Najran
Munabbi
W. Badr
Alhijrah
an-Nadir
Sa'da
Saqayn
Haydan
W. Amla
al-Aqlin
Undefined Boundary
W. Khabb
Shahara
Huth
al-Qabi
Habur
Khamir
Dhi Bin
al-Mahabisha
Jawf
Suq al-Khamis
Hajja
Iyal Yazid
Qaryat Jabal al-Milh
az-Zuhra
al-Khawba
Bani al-Awwam
Thula
at-Tur
Kawkaban
ad-Darb
Majzar
W. Mawr
at-Tawila
Ibn 'Abbas
al-Mahwit
Ma'rib
al-Haruniya
Jibal Hufash
SAN'A
al-Munira
Jibal Milhan
Bayt Baws
ad-Dahi
Khamis Bani Sa'd
Jabal Masar
Jabal Harraz
Harib
Wadi Hadramawt
Tarim
Say'un
Shibam
W. 'Amd
Sif
W. Daw'an
Ma'bar
Jabal Bura
al-Hudayda
Mansuriya
ad-Durayhimi
Jibal Rayma
Dhamar
Rada'
Utma
Towards Sayhut and al-Qishn
Dhi Ashra
as-Sawadiya
Habban
Damt
at-Taffah
Mukalla
14°
Hays
Ibb
W. Bana
al-Haqab
al-Baydha
al-Khawkha
Lawdar
Ta'izz
Jabal Sabir
at-Turba
ERITREA
Aden
Gulf of Aden
DJIBOUTI
100 km 328 ft
Desert
Coral reef
200 500 1000 2000 3000 m
656 1640 3280 6560 9840 ft
42°
46°

CONTENTS

IMPRESSIONS OF YEMEN

PREFACE

Yemen is famous the world over for the beauty and originality of its architectural styles, which bear witness to a striking accord between man and his surroundings. The great geographical diversity and difficult communications within Yemen have encouraged different architectural solutions, each adapted to its region.

The separation of the Arabian Peninsula from the African landmass gave birth to the Red Sea. An indirect consequence of this was the rising of high, steeply sloping mountains, whose summits reach almost four thousand meters (over thirteen thousand feet). The high plateaus, scored with deep valleys and scarred with lava flows, hold water from monsoons blowing across the Indian Ocean and allow a rich, varied agriculture to flourish on their terraced slopes.

Further east, the plateaus descend and bear the greatest desert on Earth, the famous Rub al-Khali, literally, the "empty quarter," for which the Bedouin also have a more spare and abrasive word—"the sands."

The Tihama, which is a hot, humid coastal plain, has much in common with nearby Africa: huts made out of plant materials; low-set houses built with small bricks; coral constructions in the major ports; and the use of moucharabies—wooden latticework balconies—as ventilation systems. In the mountainous areas, the Yemenis use local chipped stone to build houses that are amazingly tall. On the semi-arid plateaus, mud dwellings are constructed using either mudbricks or cobwork layers. Highly elaborate edifices are built despite the simplicity of the materials: in Wadi Hadramawt, some buildings are nine stories high.

In contrast to arid Arabia Petrea, Yemen is green Arabia, the Arabia Felix described by the Ancients. The etymology of the word "Yemen" contains ideas of being happy and upright, as opposed to being warped, heavy with sinister omens and impurity.

When you face east, Yemen is situated to the right of Mecca and was the "land blessed by the gods" in ancient times. It became famous not so much for its luscious green mountains as for the riches made from its caravan monopoly in the incense trade.

In fact, by the time the incense reached the shores of the Mediterranean after having spent sixty-three days on caravan—burdened with taxes, tolls, and tithes to pay all along the land route—it was worth more than its weight in gold. Incense was precious enough to have pride of place among the gifts the Queen of Sheba gave to King Solomon.

The Greeks and Romans did their utmost to find out where the production sites lay, in the hope of taking possession of them, but in vain. Alexander the Great sent lieutenants to discover if there might be a sea route, but his premature death abruptly ended the attempt. In 24 BCE, the Prefect of Egypt, Aelius Gallus, led Roman legions as far as the gates of Ma'rib, before turning back without having been able to reach the forests of rosemary and balsam trees, whose legendary existence remained mysterious, veiled in geographic uncertainty.

Once the monsoon system had been understood and a sea route discovered, the death-knell rang for the prosperity of the Southern Arabian kingdoms, whose confederation was shattered by rivalry. The Himyarite kingdoms embraced the monotheisms first of Judaism, and then with the help of the Ethiopians, of Christianity. Column capitals came across from Axum to decorate the cathedral of San'a. Today, they have been pressed into use once more in the great mosque, parts of which were built during the Prophet Mohammed's lifetime. The Yemenis are proud to recall that their conversion to Islam was brought about through the Book, and not by the sword.

Hemmed in by its mountains, Yemen remained for centuries far removed from foreign influences. The occupying Turks never managed to control the whole country. Shut in on itself, under the power of the Zaydi Imams, Yemen was preserved as a world apart. Architecture could use only local materials and thus tended to resemble the landscape, integrating itself so far into the surroundings that it came to imitate nature.

Colors from elsewhere won over the coastal plain, open to influences from across the sea; and, at the desert's edge, colors also invaded the valleys, cradles of faraway emigration. Yet the Yemen of the high plateaus dug itself in among plain, gangue stones, set with a little whitewash or plaster. The birth of the Republic in the North, in 1962, and the coming of independence to the South, in 1967, were accompanied by an opening up to foreign worlds and their technologies, imported goods, and synthetic colors.

Once the insecurity caused by tribal struggles had been forgotten, architecture transformed itself. The fortified houses clinging to the mountain—whose materials and tones they had borrowed to the point where they blended in totally—gave way to ostentatious, wide-windowed constructions, gaily painted with bright colors.

Today the unrestrained liberty of colorful compositions dazzles the distinguished severity of the older, monochrome dwellings.

FROM EARTH
TO LIGHT

After being one with Mother Earth for a time,
the house gradually leaves the ground and reaches
for the sky in search of light

*Village of Bayt Baws
in Bani Matar.
Closely fitting stones make
a wall at Maharada.*

Page 8: *A collection of water-tanks and
basins next to the great mosque of
Dhi Bin.*

Page 10: *Village of Bani al-Awwam.*

Page 11: *Terraces on Jabal Shiragui,
Hajja province.*

EXTENDING NATURE'S WORK

Where does nature's creation stop? Where does man's work begin? Using the only locally available material leads to perfect visual continuity. Solidly set into the ground of which it is made, the house becomes one with its earthly support, and extends it: the house is a swelling on the ground, an incision in the landscape. Interference is minimal: stone on rock, mud on clay, a masonry veil conceals a prehistoric cave, hides its dark mouth, and protects the hollow, inside walls.

First the rock is broken up, then put back together bit by bit. The jigsaw pieces have changed only in size, so the finished puzzle is identical to the original.

Yet there is more to it than this. It seems that the same construction plan operates at all levels, from the smallest to the biggest, soldering the works of man to the landscape in a fascinating consistency. Both the stairway path slipping through the cliffsides and the walls made by fixing big blocks in place with tiny fragments speak the same language. The mountain is transformed into a never-ending stairway whose giant steps dwindle further and further, until they slip right inside the houses. The slope is divided into tiers, the flight of stairs into steps.

Looking closely at the seeming unity of this landscape, we can discern the measure of mankind in the filigree inscriptions he has left. The house's foundation stone is either the very rock on which it sits, or the biggest, individual rock nearby that could be moved with collective help. Then, as the wall rises higher, in the absence of any scaffolding since wood is so rare, the blocks become smaller. At the base, the raw elements are roughly cut and piled up then, further up, they are carefully calibrated and aligned. Their volume becomes that of an individual load, their size that of a handspan, marked out with a little saliva by the stone-cutter, his fingers spread, palm open wide.

Terrace walls, which can be several meters high (over nine feet) when there is a steep slope, have tiered stones, going up one step at a time, so that they may be walked on. It is by the builder's submission to these constraints, shared with the rest of nature, that he constructs this culture of harmony. The law of the sky is, above all, that of the rainstorms that gully the soil and can carry away everything in their path. While waiting for cloudbursts to come, the long, patient work of preparation decides where houses will be set, and transforms the mountain.

The Yemeni high plateaus boast the greatest construction feats of the peasant-builders who, for successive generations, have sculpted the mountain, cut down the slopes, and converted them into gigantic reservoirs. Shaped like amphitheaters, these collect and hold the run-off from the rains, through a latticework of gutters, a succession of terraces, held tight in a network of receiving channels. In order to stop the slightest seepage, the smallest crack is sealed with loving care. For days on end, the coating on the holding basins is hammered and rubbed down before being polished with mutton fat. The whitewash, mixed with finely ground basalt, is enriched with an ounce of cattle brain. The stones dug up during plowing—done crisscross-style each season better to fix down the soil—are carefully placed round the edges of the field to hold back the water from its desperate flight toward the sea.

The soil carried off by storms is gathered at the bottom of the valley and brought back up in copper hods, strapped on to the backs of men, women, and beasts. This recaptured silt is then spread over all the terraces, right up to the highest, narrowest ones.

The city of Shibam, in the heart of Wadi Hadramawt, is an almost perfect square, due to the alluvium deposits forming its base. In the limited space available above the flood-risk areas, Shibam has also grown skyward, with the highest terrace sitting eight stories above the valley. The houses made of mud-coated, unfired bricks huddle together and form a continuous wall, exactly following the lie of the alluvium beds that serve as foundations.

After rain, vegetation sprouts on the mud roofs of the pillbox-like stalls in the souk. One would think that, out of some amazing politeness, the amount of natural soil borrowed to create the market were being paid back to the landscape. In the countryside, whether to gain merit or offer thanks for grace already received, pious men have built shelters for travelers, shepherds, and their flocks caught in rainstorms. These are drystone constructions, set in folds in the ground. With no opening but an arched doorway, they are actually man-made caves, pursuing the Creator's work in this world below.

Set into the very rock to which they cling, the houses at Bayt al-Reyadi dissolve into the landscape.

At ar-Rawdha, the large foundation stones reduce in size as the wall climbs higher. The windows are circled with dark rings of kitchen smoke.

Whether on a large or small scale, the same ideas prevail behind the constructive dialogue with the mineral kingdom. In this wall at Haydan, the blocks are wedged in place by fine splinters of shale; drystone stairs slide into cracks in the cliff overlooked by the fortified village of Bukur, between Kawkaban and at-Tawila.

The city of Shibam consists of four hundred houses. It forms a regular rectangle of approximately two hundred sixty meters by four hundred meters (284 x 437 yards), set in the heart of the Wadi Hadramawt. The street plan re-uses the pre-Islamic grid that dates from the site's founding in ancient times.

The high mud houses huddled closely together form a continuous wall that follows the lie of the alluvium beds.

The track at Jibal Hufash was laid in a hurry, which means that there is no retaining wall nor receiving network for rain run-off; this is threatening the stability of the slopes, patiently terraced over generations.

*Women watch over a pair of ewes who
accompany them as they gather wild herbs
among the terraces of sorghum.*

The entire mountain has been sculpted into a gigantic reservoir-amphitheater at Shahara, which collects and holds run-off from the rains. In the holding basin, the stepping-stones that allow the water to be reached, whatever its level, continue the pattern of the tiered terraces. The heavy chore of fetching water for household needs is an honor left to the women. The water-tank is a special place to meet and chat.

On the Kawkaban plateau, the man-made terraces permit the widest possible selection of crops to grow and also prevent damage caused by erosion.

In the village of Dhi Ashra, between Yarim and Damt, the holding basin is coated with gadad, *made from whitewash, finely ground volcanic clusters, and pozzolana (volcanic dust). The substance is beaten for a long time as it sets, until a smooth, polished, resistant surface is obtained. Padding is applied to the corners for greater watertightness.*

When placing the limestone pieces into the whitewash oven great care is taken so that heat circulates evenly.

WHEN WALL BECOMES LIGHT

R einforcements are called for to fight the slow erosion worked by the rain, which insidiously and relentlessly washes away the roofs and openings of the houses. A different material must be used: the secret alchemy of fire transforms charred stone into immaculate milk, into a substance that is thirstily water-absorbent before becoming water-resistant.

East of San'a, in the region of the Bani Hushaysh, Ghuraz is famous for its gypsum quarries, where the raw material is turned into a plaster called *goss*. Since wood has become ever more rare and expensive, the ovens are now oil-fired, that is when they are not burning used tires—giving off a thick smoke whose blackness is matched only by the whiteness of the end-product. These ovens, built in fireproof brick, are the shape of shortened cones, resembling miniature towers of Babel.

The whitewash made in Wadi Hadramawt is much prized because its manufacturing process is long and slow. The limestone is broken up into small pieces, piled up to form a lattice over one meter (three feet) high, allowing the heat to circulate regularly and evenly. A clay outer shell closes around the whole apparatus, and the lengthy, sealed cooking process can begin. Afterward, the charred products are reduced to powder, slightly dampened, then worked over repeatedly with giant beaters, until a fine, homogeneous paste is formed. The mixture is packaged for sale in used, twenty-liter (four-and-a-half-gallon) drums, filled to overflowing with the cone-shaped mix—proving the producer's generosity and helping the purchaser forget the high price. Added to the whitewash is wood ash, from *tannours*, the ovens in household kitchens, before it is used on the terraces. Yet this traditional technique is becoming impossible nowadays. The overconsumption of wood for heating—aggravated by using motorized vehicles to fetch firewood—and the resulting desertification have led to the generalized use of gas for cooking. Thanks to this hydraulic binder, with its

26

remarkable plasticity and resistance, the monochrome buildings, which are either all stone or all mud, earn some white braiding. The terrace-roof's waterproofing stretches up as far as the roof edging, and the coating on the wall reaches the edge of the bay opening. In these first, thrifty whitewashings, scarcely anything ventures beyond the surrounds of the openings.

A hand appears from inside and furtively explores a little further, then begins splashing all around. A line materializes, runs from one window to another, and then slides from one story to another, until it has embroidered an arresting lattice pattern, turning to white light, on the facade.

The openness of the facade is intensified by the generous plaster, or whitewash decoration, which enlarges and exaggerates the windows. With fantasy and imagination, whitewash becomes white lace and sets about emphasizing the changing stories, the terrace arches, exposes a crack in attempting to cover it up, creates a fake window for symmetry's sake, writes expiatory phrases. The wall becomes light, with only shadow to set off how perfect is the curve of an arch engraving, how exact a stylized design, how faultless the calligraphy. It may be true that these white explosions outlining the windows repel flies—as the house-owners claim—but what they do, above all, is attract attention. Their freshened whiteness cries out news of a joyful family event: the return of a pilgrim, a forthcoming wedding. Aesthetic quality transcends utility and, rich in symbols, affirms its place. While fulfilling its practical uses, the whiteness of plaster creates an inner shell that is soft and spacious, making the area seem limitless.

Inside the house, dissimulated between two floors, under a protective layer of plaster, is a little secret door, sealed off in periods of trouble; behind the door is a tiny storeroom housing rifles, jewelry, rare items, and precious objects.

There are nothing but worthy occasions for brightening the truth of pure white: on circumcision, at the end of the Ramadan fast. "God is beautiful and loves beauty," says the Koran. Beauty here takes on the appearance of light—light which is nothing other than one of the ninety-nine qualities of God.

"May God whiten your face" is the invocation uttered to follow the glorious example. This is whiteness as opposed to blackness, the latter dishonoring he who fails to obey the rules of Islam; whereas white, with its reflecting brightness is a synonym for purity and grace. Before visiting the holy places, the pilgrim dons the white *ihram*, a garment consisting of two pieces of pure cotton simply knotted together. In a spread of scree, a white trail marks the path of devotion linking the lower oratory to the high tomb of the very pious and venerated Ahmad Ibn Isa al-Muhajir, who came to Hadramawt from Iraq in the eighth century to preach the holy word. In the uniform wall formed by the houses of Thula, squeezed together at the foot of the strategic cliff, the mosque's immaculate cupola shines forth and fills with light.

The long, tedious, and exhausting work of beating the whitewash to a smooth consistency is sustained by rhyming chants as here at Shibam.

At first hugging the window surrounds and terrace edges, the whiteness of
plaster or whitewash gradually invades entire facades.
From left to right: Ralab in the Jawf, Sa'da, Saqayn, San'a Bayt Zubeiri,
Budaya in Wadi Daw'an, Helf at Jabal Gheylan.

Applying a splash of whitewash at Jibal Rayma.

At Shibam, Hadramawt, a fresh coat of whitewash protects the lower part of the walls. A chicken cage hangs above the entrance. The small hatch set on the left of the door allows the wooden key to be slid through so that it works the lock on the inside.

The application of goss *around the doors and to protect the base of the construction weaves a continuous band that joins each house to its neighbor on San'a streets.*

Pages 32–33: *White on black or black on white? The lines traced by the plaster decoration on dark stone, at Bayt Shemran in Jabal Masar, create a graphic maze whose visual balance is almost upside down. Above the windows, we can read the names God, Mohammad, and Ali: the Creator, the Prophet, and his son-in-law.*

The plaster decoration emphasizes the frieze separating the stories, the stained glass, and the joints in the masonry. The small, protruding, openwork constructions, where the water-jugs keep cool, also allow the inhabitants to see who is knocking at the door.

The mafraj, *or reception lounge, in the home of Ahmad Shabibi, San'a. The plaster coating creates a ledge, which houses all those items specially reserved for offering hospitality: candle-holders, perfume-burners,* qat *spittoons, aspergers, and vases.*

The tomb of Ahmad Ibn Isa al-Muhajir, in Wadi Hadramawt, is much visited, especially on Fridays. Similarly to many ancient, sacred places consisting of an upper and lower temple linked by a staircase, the path through this sanctuary leads the visitor up to the temples in the order of their importance.

*The mosque's cupola, which is regularly whitened, contrasts with
the monochrome harmony of the houses set at the foot of the
Thula cliff, dominated by the fortress.*

At al-Mahwit, the twin window is topped by a divided arch of ribbed foliage tightly gripping the stained glass. Special care and attention are given to growing medicinal and aromatic plants.

CONTINUOUS EVOLUTION

The house that treasures life in its heart is a living thing. If the stones, loosely balanced on the edges of the roof-terrace walls, are meant to look like projectiles in case of need, they are also a sign that the construction is unfinished, that it continues to evolve. Tradition considers that only the works of the Creator are perfect and complete.

The absence of seeds for growth, the impossibility of the house developing any further, is taken to mean that the owner is deceased and his family line has died out.

It is true that the houses keep getting bigger and changing. By livening up the plaster decoration year after year the craftsman sketches out a path of renewed imagination. The interior layouts of the big houses in the old city of San'a continually change, depending on the events that modify family organization: marriages, births, journeys, inheritance.

The visual coherence that persists in the city is due to the houses being continuously rebuilt, over the centuries, on top of earlier houses. It is therefore not unusual to find buildings whose first levels date from the seventeenth century while the last story has scarcely been completed. In the modern part of San'a, the unfinished look of the buildings has been caused, even recently, by the tax system, which stipulates that certain taxes are to be paid upon signing a declaration that a building has been completed. Needless to say, completion is put off eternally.

The inhabited stories are surmounted with pillars whose metal rods for reinforcing concrete stick up above them. These wait for work to restart once the owner's expected prosperity is realized.

This impression of almost permanent, continuous growth is reinforced with the construction technique *zabur*, widely used in north-eastern Yemen, in which beds of earth are piled up one on top of the other, seemingly endlessly, with the task never completed.

Wood is rare so, in order to do without scaffolding, the master-mason positions himself on the wall under construction and his assistants throw him balls of damp earth, mixed with chopped straw for improved adhesion. As soon as the earth-ball reaches the master-mason, he deflects it and, in one smooth movement, throws it hard on to the wall. A layer is built up, measuring one forearm length (about half a meter or eighteen inches). Then the shape is carefully patted smooth with a beater, to reduce the small cracks that have appeared while the mud was drying. The entire operation is pure ballet, sustained by singing and chants, which are often religious. Each layer of mud is allowed to dry for one or two days before the next is applied. As the wall grows higher, it follows level by level the line of pointed foundation stones, which ensures the structure's solidity.

In these areas close to the desert—hot by day and cold by night—the thick mud walls store heat during the day and release it slowly during the night, in this way to hold in the cool of the night for as long as possible.

Curled up in his lair of unbaked mud, our builder has nothing to fear, neither the burning sun nor rifle bullets, which would be stopped better by the walls than by concrete before they could explode.

Sometimes enriched with liquid manure, this gentle, organic architecture looks like that from the animal kingdom, like the secretions of termite colonies and the sticky balls holding together swallows' nests.

Yet, where else could we find such a fertile model for harmonious growth, but in ever-present nature itself, in the tree and its fruits, which contain paradise? Whoever has lain in the rustling shade of a palm tree, savoring a date that melts in the mouth, knows what the height of happiness can be! The walls too are richly covered in stylized palms, symbols of growth and renewed greenness. The tiny hanging gardens of medicinal herbs and aromatic plants on the window ledges thrive under the watchful eyes of the women. Their floral designs not only invade the expert hands that tend them, but also take over the facade of the building. These busy, skillful hands are decorated the same way, when they rest from their toil, with a myriad of floral designs.

The arches of the bay openings watch the leaves branch out and grow, like the five fingers of an open hand, while the bunches laden with berries promise coming abundance. The branches used in the ceilings take up, once more, the theme of plant growth. The sap runs through the central stem or trunk and gradually irrigates the entire plant, symmetrically and continuously. It thus creates all over a surface that has ever-increasing exchanges with water and sun.

In his impatience, the painter-builder is already drawing on the house wall the colored shadow of this tree that he has invited to come and grow nearby. As if to perfect the work, rust on the metal door has encouraged some buds from the flowering bush to open up.

On the skin, on the wall, this fertile flourishing palm celebrates life, wards off drought and invites us into a springtime world where all is green.

Open palms, open hands smooth and weave a gentle web, bringing peace.

Palms grow both on a house wall in Mahagar, Jabal Bura', and on the hand of this woman from as-Sawadiya.

The zabur *construction process is used all over the Sa'da region. Layers of earth are piled up higher at the corners, following the lie of the pointed foundation stone. The wall's stability and wind-bracing qualities are thus enhanced.*

The master-mason positions himself on the wall under construction and his assistants throw him balls of damp earth, mixed with chopped straw and a little liquid manure at Wadi Khabb.

On the palms of hands as on the metal door, stems, leaves, and flowers never stop growing. The branches on the ceiling are set out like the leaf ribs of a palm, clearly showing the dexterity required for such highly skilled work.

Pages 44–45: Between the windows of this house in Jabal Harraz, in the Manakha region, grow white palms, weaving a continuous plant-matter lattice.

In the village of Ibn 'Abbas, Hassan Ali has decorated the ceiling of his hut with a bountiful orchard. This wonderful garden filled with budding trees resembles paradise on earth.

On the trellis of the geometric decor, palm-trees, tendrils, and vines flourish, to the great pleasure of the owner Ahmad Tawbul, in the fishing village of al-Khawba.

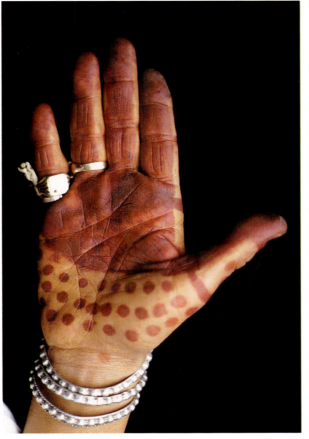

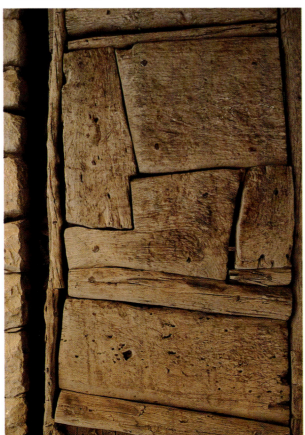

Hands colored with henna and vermilion sport architectural designs, while the sections of a door fit together like clasped hands.

*At the house of Ibrahim Darwish in the village
of al-Haruniya, the main door recess is
scarred—like an abrasion on the skin—with
three-dimensional lines, drawing a full-size
millet plant, some hearts, and a pair of scissors.*

This metal door on the outskirts of Amran and this house at al-Meshiaba, near al-Baydha, both display luxuriant plant decoration as a sign of prosperity.

AN EXTENSION
OF OUR BODY

The house shelters life, follows human movements,
and extends our body. We see our reflection
in the mirror of construction.

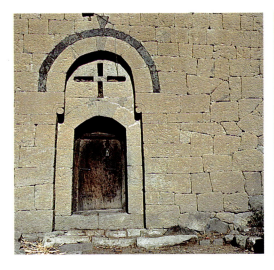

The blocks are so intimately joined, whatever their shape, that the Yemenis call this kind of masonry literally "male and female." The arch of the main door to this house, south of San'a, is emphasized by a line of basalt, whereas a stroke of kohl dramatically redraws the browbone of this little girl, near as-Sawadiya.

Page 52: The positioning of the apertures makes this facade at Alhijrah Falala look like a man.

Pages 54–55: The anthropomorphism of this mud house in the Wadi Mekzer, Jawf, does not seem to surprise the man from San'a.

THE FACE OF THE FACADE

The words used in Yemen for both the body and the house reveal the ambivalence and similarities surrounding these notions. For instance, *wahj al bayt*, "the face of the house," is used to describe the main facade, and *wahj al bab* to define the beautiful side of a door, the one that greets the visitor.

El hawi el batn, literally "the belly of the insides," means the interior courtyard of a house. The main pillar, which is the heart of the structure—a string wall round which winds the staircase of the high tower-houses—is called in San'a *al qutb*, "the backbone," and in Shibam in Hadramawt, *al arous al bayt*, "the house's betrothed."

Over and above anatomical references, words describing the constructed dwelling place and the human home often overlap. To describe what tribe a person belongs to, the words for belly (*batn*), thigh (*fakhdh*), and flesh (*luhma*), are used. *Bayt* refers as much to the house itself as to the resident family and their genealogy. These word-for-word equivalents are also found at more literary levels of language: the eyes are said to be the windows of the soul; and a porch, or a big bay opening, is described as the soul of the house.

As for language, visual associations link the facades of Yemeni houses to the morphology of the face and the make-up used to highlight it. Just as the mouth orifice, considered obscene, is concealed by the veil, so the door is protected by a deflecting wall, reinforced on the inside by a curtain. Thus, the house's hidden life is better obscured and protected, its breath held in.

The huts of the Tihama are built from branches, twisted, bound together, and coated with clay. The conical roofs are made from bundles of wild grasses gathered in the semi-desert areas lying between wadis. Tied together and fixed on, in small, overlapping bunches, these grasses provide good protection from dripping rain. The grasses are then fastened under a lattice of braided ropes, made from *doum* palm leaves, so that the whole interwoven structure offers greater resistance to the terrible winds, especially the sand-laden ones that blow in springtime. The intricate work involved in braiding plant matter into walls and roofing is similar to the technique employed for styling the girls' hair into braids all over their heads. Both men and women wear tall hats, made of plaited palm leaves, that trap large amounts of insulating air above their heads, just as do the high conical roofs.

Since the dwelling is a continuation of the body, in all its nooks and crannies we can find bodily traces: nail clippings and bits of hair wound round a stick, carefully kept after each hairdressing session. These must not be thrown to the four winds, must not fall into the hands of uncontrolled forces outside, the jealous, evil-minded, and the hordes of jinns.

As far as construction materials allow, the house bends its shape to follow the lines of the body, the curving flow of gestures and movement. These houses made from plant materials and constructed from clay are more flexible than are those made in stone and brick. Yet once stone and brick are covered over they can produce smooth-angled inside walls. Even if the right angle imposes its strict functionality on the upper floors, on the ground floor the curve reigns supreme, facilitating foot traffic where the narrow streets crisscross. A ledge formed in the interior, shaped-plaster wall turns into an open hand for holding books. Veins from the branches making up the ceiling remain visible and alive underneath their clay skin.

The strict binary rhythm of the openings slackens just enough to give a wink, and the inkling of a smile, toward the window below. A human brow ridge is picked out by the dark stone, chosen to emphasize the arch above the bay opening. Half-open shutters close like eyelids blinded by the sun's glare. Shaggy bushes above the entrance porch form a fringe of shadows. The house is looking at us.

At al-Baydha, a wall conceals the main door of the house, just as the veil hides the woman's mouth. Everything is done to protect the interior of the house from the gaze of strangers.

The construction's skeleton of layers of earth disappears beneath a clay-rich coating. The surrounds of the openings are scored with scratches whose design conceals wrinkles and cracks.

The features of this woman from Wadi Badr have been disguised behind a dry herb-based mask.

*The corner of a store in
the Habur souk.*

*The alabaster disks of the
round windows have been
replaced by a collection of
dry stones.*

Black stones emphasize the arch windows of this Dhamar palace, as a line of kohl highlights the browbone of these made-up little girls from the al-Baydha region.

Here the essential opening has received strategic reinforcement: the main door to this mud house in Ma'bar is made of carefully matched stones. The design created by the spaces, between the door and the relieving arch, is reminiscent of the tattoo ornamenting the center forehead of this Bedouin woman from Wadi Majzar.

In the at-Tur region and the piedmont of Wadi Mawr, young women style their hair in a plait framing the temples.

The covering of this hut, in the az-Zuhra region, is strengthened by a latticework of ropes in order better to resist the wind. The binding between the roofing and the wall forms a peripheral braid.

Radiant decoration and make-up for this door near al-Baydha and the face of this woman at the Salous souk, Wadi Badr.

FROM EYE MAKE-UP TO WINDOWS

Applied inside the house, the plaster whitewash flicks round a window opening, creating the window's eye make-up. Eyes are lined with kohl, windows edged with whitewash. Over and above the usual reasons given for using kohl and plaster—their antiseptic properties, protection against cracks and leaks—what remains most striking is the enhanced beauty of the eye and the visual impact of the apertures in the facade.

There certainly is magnetism in this charcoaled enlargement of the eyes, designed to discourage looks of desire and ward off the evil eye.

Protection is the essential function of these decorations which, like masks, hide the true features under a picture puzzle of lines, diverting the eye into a maze of inextricable arabesques.

Green make-up is obtained by squeezing liquid from plants rich in sap, such as the *Papilionaceae*, pod-producing plants, which have astringent properties and close skin pores. The woman crushes their leaves in the palm of her hand then, with one or more fingers of the right hand—the left hand, considered impure, is kept for intimate hygiene —she makes up her face, intuitively and imaginatively.

Some women apply this make-up only directly around the eyes, while others continue the circling movements and draw a band right across their face to form a carnival eye-mask. Still others make up the entire face and then, with their fingernails, draw streaks. And lastly, some use a twig or a match and carefully make designs with dots and lines.

The design is done as much by removing make-up as by adding more and, whatever the motif, the eye area receives a lot of attention. Doubtless, the skin here is more fragile, but the ultimate aim is to ward off any possible harm that the evil eye might intend. The dominant theme, however, comes back to "shades," to protect the eyes from the gaze of others, "sunglasses" to protect from the glare of the sun.

Demonstrating close bonding and affection, friends will sport the same design or apply each other's make-up.

Women often keep in the fold of their turban, stiffened with a piece of old cardboard wrapping, a little box with a mirrored lid so that they can easily touch up their make-up. Imaginative make-up is created by the women from the rural areas of northwest Yemen every time they venture out of the house and face the dangers beyond. Once back in the protective safety of the house, the make-up comes off with a little water. The use of this fleeting finery is reminiscent of how city women use the veil.

To complement the make-up, hair is adorned with aromatic herbs: sagebrush, basil, or rue give a woman a continuously fine scent, which, among other virtues, is said to ward off evil spirits.

Underneath the colorful yet enigmatic design, the face's true identity becomes indecipherable. The profound strength and force of this decorative second skin is that it flattens, erases the real face and conceals it behind colored patterns. The feminine face, thus disfigured, dematerialized by the abstract network of lines, colors, streaks, and slashes, now escapes cupidity. Hidden beneath its make-up, the face is no longer exposed to the dangers of the outside world, it is safe from sexual desire and jealousy.

As a mirror reflects an image by inverting it, this need to hide behind paint achieves its aim through a more agreeable inversion: the remodeling exercise attracts as much as it repulses, beautifies as much as it masks. Thus, these pictorial games are full of contradictions: concealing oneself by becoming more noticeable and attracting attention by trying to hide.

On examination, the whole phenomenon is richly ambiguous. Whether these apparent scribbles look rough or subtle, improvised or carefully executed, if they mask the body, they also reveal the personality of their designer.

Is this pure chance or knowledgeable research? Quite clearly, the multiple reasons behind these infinite designs are woven in the subconscious. Casual resemblances clearly show the unspoken agreement linking human beings, their appearance, and their homes.

The liquid from a plant rich in sap, from the Papilionaceae, *pod-producing family, is squeezed into the left hand. The woman uses first a finger from the right hand, then a small stick, to draw on a protective make-up before leaving the house.*

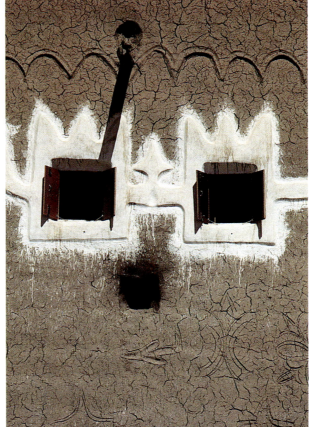

*A red pompom tops an obscure mask at Munabbi; a red star sets
beneath the shadowy window opening in at-Turba.*

*Framing eyes and apertures: a woman in the Khamis Saqayn souk
and windows at al-Buga, Wadi Alaf.*

Pages 70–71: *A painted carnival mask frames the eyes; a painted
frame outlines the window.*

*At Wadi Wahal, the make-up line runs
over the cheek, underlining the eyes.*

*Near Huth, two lines of colored stones run above the openings,
emphasizing relieving arches and lintels.*

On the face and on the facade of Utma souk, applying color demonstrates great creative liberty allied to a search for chromatic harmony. Turbans, jewelry, make-up, and headwear—each item of protective disguise is carefully chosen.

The framework concealed beneath the cement coating reappears in the colored design of the joints. The lattice thus created is enriched by superimposed motifs. The six-pointed star is drawn in Yemen as the sign of Solomon, and not as the star of David. The colored make-up mask hides the features of the face, at Wadi Badr.

As though she had wished to dissolve into the vegetation surrounding her, this woman from Wadi Badr has chosen a dress and make-up whose floral design provide perfect camouflage.

IN THE SHELTER OF COLOR

To be in the shelter of color, is this not taking to extremes (to the point of foolhardiness) the tranquillity of living? This is the question Bachelard asks the robin in his *Poetics of Space*. Painting one's body and painting one's house express a similar wish: for completeness, self-protection, and the ability to seduce.

The palette of colors used is vast and has increased with the addition of imported, synthetic products. Depending on the area, women exploit local, natural resources or purchase the ingredients they need to make their colored masks.

Orangey-yellow is obtained from turmeric roots, pulverized on a stone mill then mixed with water.

Black comes from many different sources: antimony; psilomelane (a manganese oxide); a mixture of indigo and ash; a plant tar obtained by slowly burning an oleaster (wild olive); or a chemical dye.

The red used is a metal oxide, lepidocrocite or goethite, found locally in flake form, then powdered and blended with various additives: dried rosebuds; shells; sesame, almond, or apricot oil; or cardamom. The exact recipe remains the well-kept secret of a few women, who prepare it for sale in small, solid cones for mixing with water.

The indigo plant, which used to be grown traditionally, especially in the al-Baydha and Wadi Zabid areas, is scarce nowadays. As well as dyeing the skin, indigo also protected it from the harmful effects of the sun and from parasites. The plant was very popular with the soldiers of the Imam, whose shiny indigo turban was a rallying sign for the Bedouin men and women of the north. This much prized blue-black is used as a substitute by the women of the Sayhut region, on the shores of the Indian Ocean. They coat their faces with it, then wrap their heads in a veil that hangs over all round like a large visor. All is covered and protected, and even the teeth are crowned with gold.

Inside the house, the areas that get most dirty are painted first and foremost, areas where people pass most or rub against surfaces: the entrance hall, stairway, the lower parts of the walls in the reception rooms against which people lean when they are seated. The massive masoned blocks making up the kitchen abandon their sooty blackness in favor of a colorful, shiny gloss, which hugs the curves better than tiles would. The synthetic glosses shine so brightly and are so simple to apply that they are fierce competition for the traditional wall-coverings, the long work of the *gadad*—a kind of cement—with its honey tones.

Green, the color of Islam, is applied everywhere. Evoking unspoiled abundant vegetation, it brings comfort and coolness in a world constantly assailed by drying light. The teahouse, an oasis amid the city's dusty streets, attracts passers-by with its solid green wall and beckons them inside to cool off in its soothing, shady interior. The newer restaurants and cafés invite you to pass beyond their aluminium windows to take refreshment in front of a huge picture of the Swiss Alps, teeming with green grass, flowers, and tumbling waterfalls.

The wall-hangings complete this composition of carpets, cushions, arm- and head-rests. They spin a multicolored cocoon to curl up in, abandoning oneself to feelings of delight. Carpets—symbols of exchange and interchange between the nomadic and sedentary worlds—are often the only furnishings in reception rooms, being used simultaneously as seats, beds, and tables.

In the big houses of Tarim, the piled up layers of Persian rugs demonstrate the mobililty and wealth of these foreign traders.

Yet mishaps multiply and, on the most garishly colored, printed velours, you can see religious and trivial designs freely and indistinctly mixed. There are illustrations of, for instance, the Ka'ba in Mecca, dogs smoking and playing billiards, a bearded Christ showing his sacred heart, Snow White and the seven dwarfs, a stag belling among does quenching their thirst under a fiery sunset.

As for the choice of designs that have no immediate bearing in Yemeni symbolic thought, it seems likely that the carpet-collectors were attracted by the explosive colors.

In the at-Tur region, the women prepare a fragrant cosmetic powder by finely grinding mineral pigments with cardamom, dried roses, pieces of shell, and apricot stones. The precious mixture is delicately picked up with a feather.

In the dihliz, *or entrance hall, to the house of Mohammed bin Qassim, in San'a, the central arch reaches two stories high, allowing a set of scales to be hung for weighing grain and other goods before they are put away in the adjoining store-rooms. The small staircases lead to rooms traditionally reserved for guards and servants in big houses.*

Every afternoon, in the mafraj, *or reception room, of this
at-Tawila house, there is a gathering to chew* qat, *appreciated for
its qualities as a tonic and mood enhancer. A printed tapestry
protects the wall, extending the backrest cushions.*

At Mukalla, the freshness of light green invites the passer-by to come and sit awhile over a glass of tea.

To protect their faces, the women of Sayhut apply indigo, then cover their heads with a scarf, which they tie very far forward so that only a narrow opening remains.

This couple from Wadi Yahar positively gleam with a shared passion for shining colors. Their preference for the brightness of gold is expressed as much in their choice of clothes as in their investment in dental work. The red of the woman's beauty mask continues on to her dress and the fringes of her headdress.

The make-up box cut out of a block of steatite, or soapstone, is
protected by spiral basketwork ornamented with cowries and
strapped with fringed leather, as here in the as-Sawadiya region.
The name given to this apparatus is husn, *meaning "beautify."*

The contrast between the intensely red mask, so thick that it is cracking, of this little girl from the as-Sawadiya region and the black of her pupils, emphasized by redrawn eyebrows, creates a spectacular effect.

A hut interior in the Wadi Mawr region. The clay coating creates a composition of ledges that turn into shelves and recesses. The pegs that stick out of the horizontal supports are both ornamental and functional, used for restraining or hanging up objects, especially baskets.

A LARGE GARMENT

When the woman leaves home, her face hidden
beneath the veil, does she not take a little of
the house's protection with her?

A penchant for black and yellow stripes, on the cardigan as well as the house, in the village of Ayda, in Wadi Mawr.

Page 88: The dark limestone of the houses in al-Mahabisha serves as a support for fine plaster decoration, made up of friezes of chevrons, diamonds, zigzags, and broken or continuous lines, like so many embroidered designs.

Pages 90–91: White and earth tones color this house in al-Aqlin, Wadi Amla, and another in Saqayn with splashed apertures. The shades also match the house-owners' choice of clothing.

THE ENCLOSURE WEARS A VEIL

Before becoming the cloth covering the body and face of the Muslim woman, the *hijab* was a fabric wall in the tent separating the family section, reserved for the women, from the public section, where guests were welcomed. In order to preserve domestic privacy, Mohammad had a separate canvas section installed in his Medina house, which also became the first mosque. He was moved to do this by the harassment of prying visitors, who continued pursuing him even on his wedding night. He wanted to make the women of the community easily identifiable by the opponents of the new religion who pestered them and tried to take advantage of them in the dark, narrow little streets. Thus the Prophet, borrowing from aristocratic tradition, instituted the veil as a mark of distinction and protection.

From the outset, the dual nature of the veil was established, as a sign of both recognition and protection. However, in its ability to erase the personality and bring anonymity, the veil was challenged by she whom Tradition states was Mohammed's favorite wife, Aisha. She asked: "God has given me beauty to share; why should I hide it?" Owing to its powers of concealment, the veil was thus to hide a world of seduction.

The double meaning still persists: garment and tent wall.

Using the same words, you may talk about black tents and actually mean women in their black *sharshaf*, Cairo-style, or you may describe traditional Bedouin encampments with their tents woven from black goat hair.

These goat-black houses turn white in springtime when the abundance of milk allows cheeses to be made, which are then set to dry on the tent awning. White thus signifies abundance.

Rarer and more precious colors are reserved for decorating the partition between the women's section and the reception area, which is open to all and concealed by nothing. The tent partition is made by sewing together strips of cloth, each a forearm's width to correspond to an easy back-and-forth shuttle movement on the Bedouin woman's individual, horizontal loom.

If the design is inspired by current techniques, it quickly takes on an important, aesthetic, and independent strength. The decoration on the mud houses takes up, and so underlines, the geology of the clay layers in the houses themselves. The oxidized ochre, gathered in the clay quarries, is stabilized with cattle or camel urine. The application of alternate, contrasting bands of beige and ochre make the building appear larger, according to a widespread principle that was used for instance during the Italian Renaissance.

In the Hays region of the Tihama, the bodices of women's dresses are designed around three or four small pieces of brocade or printed fabric, selected for their complementary and contrasting color tones. The precious fragments are cut into strips then put back together in alternating patterns to enhance their decorative effect.

Similarly, the painter-builders clothe house facades with wide horizontal bands of alternating, remnant colors.

The Tihama weavers stretch out their horizontal looms on the sand itself and group together colored chain threads in alternating bands of varying widths, with an obvious preference for red and gold. The alliance systems and heraldry behind these stripes, from which each clan, each lineage takes its signs of recognition and belonging, as for Scottish kilts, are still to be written down.

The weaves of the south boast violets, Tyrian pinks, raw greens—favorite color harmonies that were produced in the cotton-mills of the British Indian Empire.

These same striped fabrics, or *jihaf*, woven in the villages around Bayt al-Faqih, ad-Durayhimi, or in India, are used for different purposes depending on their length. As *futa*, the Tuhamat Qahtan wear them draped over the lower part of the body, like loincloths, drawn in at the waist and reaching down to the knees for men and right to the ankles for women.

This very same cloth is used for bags to carry fodder, grain, or purchases made at the market, then when required turns into sleeping bags or hammock cradles for newborn babies. It is also pressed into service for making the cushions that garnish the high, woven-rope beds. Their colored streaks brighten the alcoves where they are piled up while guests are awaited.

The same fabric, the same design, for the body or the house.

The weavers of ad-Durayhimi are renowned throughout the Tihama. The chain threads are set out in alternate bands of color. The width of the cloth requires a team of two to pass the shuttle back and forth.

Knitting is a source of personal income for women. Their finished work is rarely sold at market, but more often at women's gatherings. Knitting is a recent technique here, and knitters use brightly colored, chemically dyed, imported wools.

This facade of a recently built house in Mansuriya, in the Tihama, blends white openwork partition, made of locally precast cement shapes and brieze blocks, with undercoat and paint. The lattice shutters and apertures help ventilate the rooms and reduce heat conduction through the walls.

The face veil of the women of San'a, the maghmuq, is decorated with concentric, red and white circles on a black background, obtained by partial dyeing, or tie-dyeing. The ties that held the cloth during immersion in the dye are drying on a stone next to the store, while freshly dyed veils are spread out to dry. Veils were traditionally made of silk but are now increasingly made of rayon.

The alternating bands of ochre and white repeat and strengthen the construction design of mud layers piled up on top of each other. This decoration enhances the visual impact of the house and seems to make it seem larger than it is.

*At Hays, the women's dresses are brightened up
with a colored bodice, consisting of alternate bands of
embroidered or printed cloth.*

*In the village of Hays, the design on the bodice and
the paint on the facade use the same geometric
and graphic principle of colored bands.*

During the Id el Kebir festivities, the men of the Munabbi tribes come to dance together in a circle, wearing striped futas. *Men from the same family line choose the same design.*

In the recess set in the thick wall, the cushions are covered with a striped cloth, which has many uses. It figures as much in furnishings as clothing, and is even used to carry loads. The bench-beds are set all around the room, as in the mafraj *for guests of the high plateau houses. However, here in the Tihama, at al-Khawkha, the high seats in tightly woven rope allow air to circulate.*

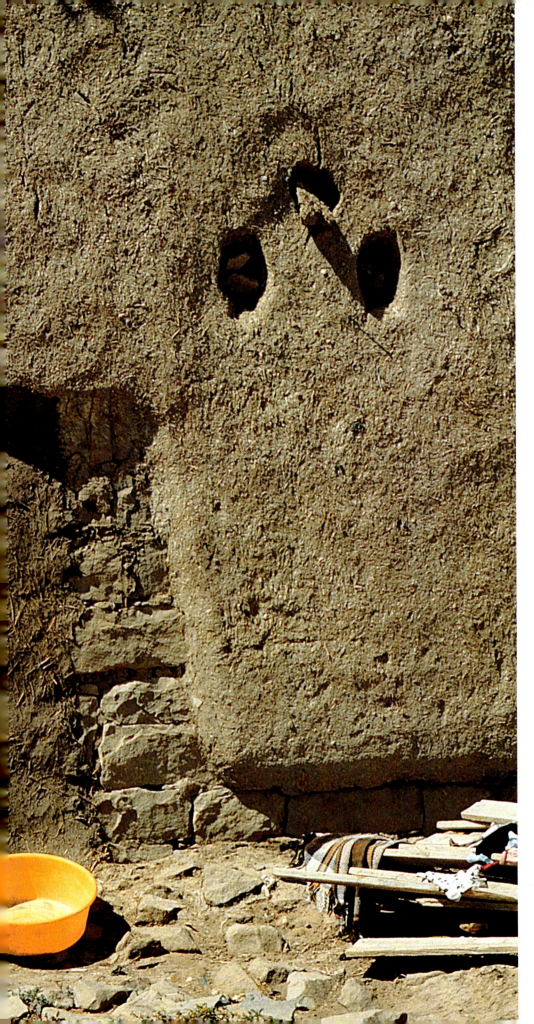

With arms outstretched in the doorway, the woman who has just donned her veil is about to leave the protective enclosure of the family home. At Rada', houses are made from mudbricks, apart from the door surround, which is constructed from stone for greater solidity.

In the village of Bani Mure, in Jabal Harraz, the chevron design appears right across the stone layers, creating on the facade a lattice as regular as crochet.

A WALL OF EMBROIDERY

A fine padding reinforces the opening cut in the partition wall, just as a buttonhole is stitched round to "heal up" the slit in the fabric. The material is double thickness at the most strategic points in the house, as fabric is hemmed on a garment.

Double backstitched leggings are worn to protect the calves from thornbushes during mountain walks right to the edge of ravines to collect fodder, wood, and branches. Embroidery runs first around the wrists, then the collar, before taking possession of the dress bodice. The wall is strengthened by the garland running along its top, around its corners, and finishing where the wall ends, just as a piece of cloth is hemmed by its edge and fringes. The lintels and doorjambs are clothed with bricks which project out in steps, so that the extra width catches and breaks up the light.

Once the structural framework is in place, drawings and designs begin filling in the interior surfaces. There is an endless choice of reversible, modular, geometric, decorative designs. Inspiration from the plant kingdom is stylized into elements that can grow on a frieze. Oblique segments double to form parallel lines that cross in spikes and diamonds. The intersection point stretches up with the height of the stone layer. The thicker, reinforced areas abound with spirals, flowery designs of petals and sepals, and brightly colored seals.

As the design begins to cover most of the support, the undrawn areas compose another drawing of their own, supplanting the pattern around them, with much poised impertinence—considering that they have made no effort to achieve this. This inversion—like the magic of black and white photo negatives—provides two perspectives, a choice of mirror-images. The line of whitewash on the black chalk becomes a dark line on pure white. These forgotten areas, untouched or left empty, enjoy considerable importance—up until the frenzy to expand takes hold once more, whereupon they disappear beneath an invading design. The developing design line rolls back the boundaries of the surface area, which fades away under the decoration and dematerializes. This decoration, which has been extended to saturation point, leads the eye astray: first, the gaze is lost in a maze of lines, then it contemplates arabesques, finds focus points for meditation.

The twisting, interlaced designs all over a mosque's dome transform the constructed object into an infinite sky, uniting the whole community of believers. The *mihrab*, the recess indicating the direction of the Ka'ba, is decorated on the side toward which the faithful prostrate themselves. The intermingled lines make the curve of the wall disappear. Similarly, the line of men praying continues on to infinity.

In the southern Tihama, the city of Zabid is famous for its university, where algebra is said to have been invented in the ninth century. The buildings are made of *tub*, or fired bricks, which are small, square—measuring a handspan (twenty-two centimeters or nine inches) by three fingers thick—and limewashed better to reflect the unrelenting glare of the sun's rays.

Using just a brick cut in two, which creates a recess in the facade, all manner of decoration is possible. With this simple starting point—one brick recessed, another protruding—a patchwork of embroidery develops over the facades: ribbons, garlands, braiding, piping, and chain-stitching.

The blacksmith's skill in soldering the bars of the gate, making the metal stronger and more rigid, is matched only by the embroideress with her needle.

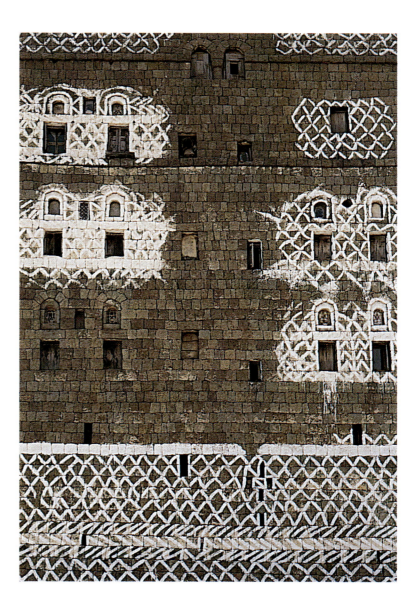

The base and the area surrounding the apertures—those places that can be reached without scaffolding—are the parts of a house usually favored for decoration.

Although there are several mountain ranges between them, the dress and make-up of this little girl from Jabal Gheylan and the store door in Bayt Ganes, Jabal Harraz, share a design based on embossed floral motifs.

Both the painted beam ceiling in this Tihama house, and the dress of this woman from Jabal Sabir, have made the most of complementary colors—blue with red and gold—in a composition of circles, punctuated by beds of flowers with radiating petals.

The women from Jabal Sabir,
which overlooks Ta'izz, take their
produce to market themselves. Every
Sunday, the Wadi Zabab souk
attracts a great many customers.
The chain-stitching overlay, worked
by machine, reinforces and decorates
the bodice and neckline of their
clothes.

These metal doors protect small stores in the Utma souk.
The sheet metal is strengthened and made rigid
by a series of bars and folded, soldered parts,
which form a design, picked out by the paint.

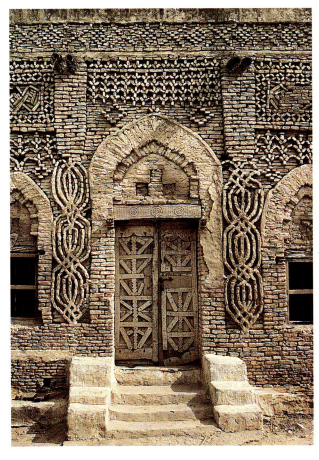

Like embroidery, the brick decoration enriches the main door of a fine house in ad-Dahi, and the windows of the palace-fortress in az-Zura.

A brick house and an embroidered dress in the al-Mansuriya souk share the same vertical arrangement of bud motifs.

A COAT-OF-ARMS

The house is the highly colored showcase for its
owner's success. At one and the same time, it expresses his
individuality and affirms his membership of the community:
a protective, as much as an attractive, parade armor.

At Bin Humeidan, in Wadi Autla, the sound of the door closing in the exterior wall reverberates in the pattern of alternating lines.

Page 112: *The white decoration of this facade at Bayt Shemran, Jabal Masar, is the pride of its owners, a symbol of abundance and vitality for the whole family.*

Page 114: *In San'a, the plaster decoration emphasizes the brickwork. The horizontal friezes, which mark the different floors, employ a very wide repertoire of oblique segments.*

Page 115: *In Jabal Masar, the facade of a Bayt Shemran house proves the graphic richness of the master-builders.*

FROM INSIDE TO OUTSIDE

At the frontier between the outside world and the inside, doors and windows concentrate attention and symbols. These openings are surrounded with preventive rituals, to allow only beneficial influences to flow into the house and ward off malevolent ones. Doors and windows are protective filters, which must control external elements: wind, sun, rain, and even more importantly intruders and baleful glances.

Protected behind its thick walls, the house is a fortress. The entrance door is low. In the finest properties, there is a small door cut inside the main one, which obliges visitors to lower their heads to enter, as though they were bowing to the master of the house, or at least to the Master of Heaven. At the house's lower levels, the openings are only narrow slits, giving a little light to stores and barns. Any intruder managing to force his way into the house would first be hampered by the semi-darkness.

As we go higher up the tower-house, the apertures become bigger. The first floors are usually given over to the women and children, while the upper floors house the reception rooms including, at the top, the *mafraj* where friends are entertained—a place for comfort and relaxation, as the Arabic root of this word suggests.

In San'a, there is a rope running through the different stories, which allows the door to be opened without anyone having to go downstairs. A coded number of bangs of the doorknocker gives the universal message "It's me," with no need for a name to be given.

The southern Arabian town-house protects family privacy by the clever way that openings are pierced in the facade.

A very functional system categorizes windows into three kinds, depending on needs: views, light, and ventilation. These different kinds of aperture allow light into rooms while, if necessary, preventing the inhabitants from being seen by the neighbors.

Viewing windows—rectangular in shape and set at the height of someone sitting cross-legged on the floor—were traditionally a set of wooden shutters, at a time when glass was rarely used in buildings. Inside the largest of these wooden shutters would be small, moving doors, often with added grills, which made it easy to vary minutely how far they opened. Light-giving windows always had, at the top, two disks of alabaster, one on top of the other, which would soften the light without reducing it. In many houses, these disks have been replaced by stained glass, consisting of colored glass pieces set in a perforated plaster grill. This multicolored stained glass, sometimes double thickness, distills sunlight into a veritable kaleidoscope.

On either side, there are *shagush*, the little ventilation openings. Stairways, hall-ways, and kitchens have overhanging windows so that the occupants can watch the street or put out pitchers to cool, and in the walls slits have been pierced to let in dappled light and extract smoke. The whole forms an enigmatic, three-dimensional picture puzzle that, in its seeming disorder, proclaims membership of a community, a family's prosperity, and a craftsman's skill.

While protecting the building from contractions and fissures, from the possible damage that could occur as materials alter, the plasterer celebrates the house's structure and its metamorphosis into spontaneous overflows, joyfully splashing the brickwork.

Thus, with identical materials and a limited decorative repertoire, every house is both similar to and different from its neighbor: each pair of houses forms a united whole that is nevertheless full of variety. Each facade is a phrase, linking to the next, until they together compose an epic poem recited across the city.

A passer-by may be offered a drink without being allowed into the area reserved for the family—the *haram*—the sacred and thus protected enclosure: beside the front door, there is a little shelter that holds a pitcher of cold water, regularly replenished.

The foundations thicken the base of the wall, thus creating a buttress which protects from water erosion and is partially dug out near the door. Here, a bench is installed, so that peddlers and tradesmen may lay down their loads and be received—in everybody's eyes and in within everyone's sight—in good faith and honesty, without ever crossing the threshold.

Firmly put up near the door are two breasts to discourage gossip and underpin fertility. These designs can be so stylized that they become obscure, and yet they signify, like a coat-of-arms, the honor of a house; they bloom with all the vigor of an inscription of atonement.

Here is traditional hospitality, courtesy of the house: at Ibb, the threshold provides the visitor or passer-by with a place to rest in the shade; at an-Nadir, cold water is on offer.

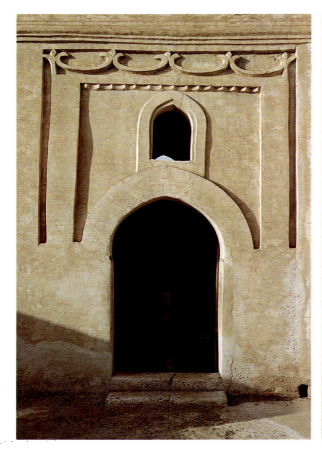  

*The main door always receives special architectural attention;
even if modest it may also be refined. The variety of styles
shown here illustrates the great regional diversity.
From left to right: ad-Durayhimi, at-Tawila, at-Tawila,
Bani Baqr, Abyan, and al-Khawkha.*

120

At Bayt Shemran, Jabal Masar, the whitewashed door decoration is enriched with protective inscriptions: on the embossment reads the devoted inscription, "God's will."

*In the village of Hamel, Bani Matar, the
entrance is guarded by prophylactic symbols:
a pair of breasts set into the stone invoke
fertility and prosperity for the house
and its inhabitants.*

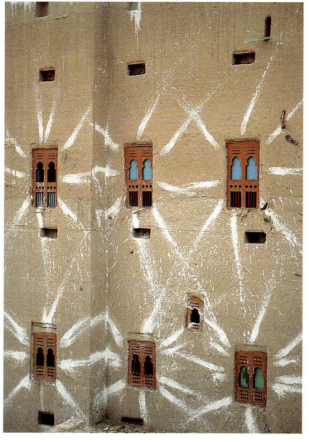

Bursting out from inside through the windows, rays of plaster splash over the facade, preventing cunning spirits from entering.

Top right: Haydan.
Bottom left: Sa'da region.
Bottom right: Alhijraj Falala.

Top left: in Wadi Amd, a sandal set into the mud coating symbolizes the foot of the Prophet, known for his protective benevolence.

The exterior wall of the great mosque at Huth conceals its austerity beneath a decoration of generous curves.

The larger-than-life design of white joints serves as a firm framework for the facade decoration at Shurman, in Wadi Yahar (left), and at Lawdar (right).

In the vicinity of Khamir, the decorative black stone set in white gives no quarter in stating its contrasts. Beneath the crowning frieze, four vertical lines and one horizontal form God's name. A wooden dove is perched on top of the dark windows.

The snake has settled at the corner of the house to watch over the inhabitants and vigilantly ensure their safety, at Hamel, Bani Matar.

PARADING FOR PROTECTION

Parading: the double-game is clearly announced. It means both showing off to attract and practicing fending off enemy blows. In tribal Yemen, they used to count regions and villages not in numbers of households or inhabitants, but in how many rifles they could muster. In fact, any man old enough to give life assumes the right to take life and to defend his honor, that of his family, and those he must protect. In order to avoid the excesses that such a practice might lead to, there is very powerful social control to minimize bloodshed. The ancient *lex talionis*—an eye for an eye, a tooth for a tooth, a life for a life—gives the group solidarity and makes it responsible for the acts of each of its members. The cycle of revenge stops only when there is arithmetical equality or agreement, after arbitration, on the payment of blood money to repair the grievance.

So, even if arms are generally carried outside the cities, on the high plateaus, their use is limited and wisely controlled by everyone. The action of one man engages the responsibility of the whole community. Symbolic of a responsible, free man, the wearing of the *janbiya*, a dagger with a curved blade, has become a symbol of Yemenihood. The rifle is gradually giving way to the automatic pistol, whose effectiveness is a token of modernity and respect.

This immoderate passion for weapons, as characteristic of virility, goes hand in hand with a highly developed sense of independence and honor. Martial qualities are ostentatiously displayed on the inside and outside walls of houses, where the proliferation of daggers and kalashnikovs attests their owners' consummate bravery and intrepid courage. Hunting trophies sit in pride of place, at the four corners of the sheikh's house. These spoils from ritual hunting of the ibex tell of the stamina, cunning, and valor of the men of the tribe; the trophies' ring-ridged, recurved horns are so many sharp points for the evil eye to come and be blinded upon.

At the end of the long civil war in the North (1962–69), between the Imam's supporters and the republicans, the birth of the new state was celebrated with great flourishes of paint, as hasty as they were generous: fighter plane fuselage markings, bombs, and missiles with victorious emblems. The joyous feeling of belonging to a nation, a republic, which had overcome obscurantism, was spontaneously displayed, and somewhat encouraged by the authorities. To brighten up the souk for the national day, the administrators made the merchants paint the doors of their little stores black, white, and red—the colors of the republic—and add green stars, which blew away when unity came on 22 May 1990.

The republican eagles that thrived, in two disguises, on either side of what used to be a frontier are, well and truly, the same species, since their descendants are everywhere: with their straight or curved wings and dominating, piercing gaze, first to the right then to the left. The strength of the symbol has taken root in the language, with the same word being used for both the royal bird, with its powerful wingspan, and for "he who is victorious": *nasr*. A sign that it upholds the values of the nation, to which it is proud to belong, the eagle prudently nests in the most unexpected places: in the cover of a spare tire, or a wash handbasin in a restaurant.

The gates are bedecked with ferocious felines, indeed with an entire protective bestiary, suggesting the combative qualities of the house-owners, whom they guard. Do not be misled by the awkward drawings: these hesitant spots are indeed the hyena's cunning camouflage, surmounted by a pair of razor-sharp fangs. For maximum security, there is sometimes a line of writing added below the drawing, since words too can weave a protective screen. "Herein lives a serpent," it warns, at the entrance to the house stores, to discourage prowlers from any attempt to lay their hands on other people's possessions. Snakes, which can slip between stones and live in communication with underground spirits, are known to provide houses with deadly effective protection. Their fatal strength and their ability to hide makes them the most-favored allies. The snake lies coiled in sculpted stone, or cast into the protruding metal fixed into the corner of the wall; it stands guard, with its specially sharpened tongue, over the inhabitants, whom it recognizes, and watches out for intruders, whose treachery it can unmask.

Decoration is not only the imprint of a people's imagination, in search of all that is good; it also provides defensive strength. Decoration builds up complex protective strategies. Thus, the drawings of automatic pistols and shells affirm the combatants' valor, whereas the eagle of the victorious republic and the dove of peace nest on the same door, which guards the barnyard. The soldier, who has borrowed his uniform from the leopard and his ferocity from the lion, keeps watch night and day, in blazing sun as in pouring rain. If you look at him for too long, you can read on his lips: "Move along there, nothing to see!"

The two gold cats, face-to-face, guarding the door to this house at San'a, were inspired by heraldic figures. The drawings of hyenas, at Watan al-Shai'b, were created from living models: those that haunt the area around Wadi Ammla, preying on cattle.

Oiled hair is held in place by leather bands, and brightened up with silver and crowns of aromatic herbs. These tribesmen from the Munabbi region, whose long hair symbolizes their status as free, courageous adults, always have a smile—and their kalashnikovs—at the ready.

Beneath the signature "al-Hajj Mohammad, blacksmith, and his sons,"
the door defends the little store with all the dissuasive force
of a pair of automatic pistols.

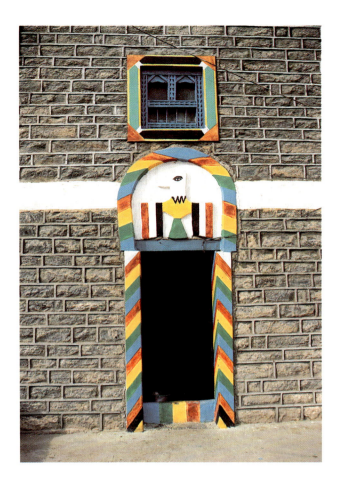

Republican eagles, however awkwardly they may be portrayed, never lose their symbolic strength. They prove the indestructible patriotism of the citizen builders. This attachment to republican values can be seen as much in the souk (next to the door) at Khamis Bani S'ad, in the north of the country, as at Bani Baqr (above) in the south.

133

The house parades a fearsome arsenal and protective bestiary:
a heavy-collared mastiff, a bomber, and assault rifle at al-Haqab, near Damt;
a missile and a fighter airplane at as-Suwayda.

In the defense parade beware of: a snake, coiled as here at San'a; eagles
perched on the lintel of the main door, or the door to the household stores, at
Bani Baqr; a pair of eagles face-to-face, among the more aggressive brush
strokes at the al-Juma souk; another eagle clutching a snake in its talons, as
seen on ancient Greek coins; and an elite soldier in leopard disguise, near
at-Taffa.

"This drawing was done to commemorate 13 June," reads the
inscription over a store in the Utma souk. The anniversary referred to
is that of 13 June 1974, when the popular Ibrahim al-Hamdi came to
power. The republican eagle and the dove of peace are depicted together
with the olive branch to celebrate the welcome, republican peace.

These doors have been freshly painted in the colors of the
national flag, to celebrate the Revolution of 26 September 1962.
It is before such a colorful backdrop that these men from
Manakha are exchanging news and this veiled woman from
San'a is bargaining with the jeweler.

A republican soldier stands guard twenty-four hours a day,
seven days a week, bringing military security to San'a;
similarly, the man from Jawf is never without his weapon.

People seek a vast range of different kinds of protection. A household's defensive kit includes: the Islamic inscription "God's will," the Yemeni dagger with a curved blade, and the snake that shoots out its sharp head to blind the evil eye, holding up a chain to trap it.

Children use a wooden dagger until they are old enough to carry a real weapon, which gives an official stamp to their status as free, responsible men.

The house of Shueh Sale, in the village of 'Ayda, Wadi Mawr, was decorated by the painter Bilal. Fixed on the wall—between a basketwork mat and the recess for cups and bowls—is a support for sweetmeats, made of superimposed stars.

THAT FAMOUS HOSPITALITY

The constraints of the mountainous landscape make communication difficult. Traditionally, the country has been divided into parcels of tribal territories, which the republican government is trying hard to make disappear. An outsider to the tribe is, at first, a stranger perhaps harboring danger, but he is also a bearer of news. Sharing bread and salt with him is the first and wisest step to take when you want to obtain information and prevent any hostile acts. Bedouin law states that, while there remains in your guest's body a morsel of the food you shared, he cannot under any circumstances use his weapon, for fear of general disgrace and exile.

As well as defusing the danger of latent violence, the meal eaten together also re-inforces community solidarity. Mutual help is the rule. In the cobwork houses of the north-west, each story consists of six or seven layers of mud, each a forearm's length high. The custom is for the owner to build the first and the last band of each floor, the others being constructed by related families in the village. Should a family fail to carry out its duty to provide mutual help, whether by accident or out of forgetfulness, that family's punishment is to lay on a banquet for the whole village.

When the construction work is finished, one or more animals are sacrificed and the blood spilled used for the prophylactic unction and atonement of the sides and lintel of the front door. Then a large meal is provided for all who helped with the building, as a return deed for their labor.

The house is designed for offering hospitality to guests. The space is organized in such a way that room can immediately be made for a newcomer, even if everyone has to hud-dle closer on the mattresses and carpets that are used as much at mealtimes as for reading, sleeping, or welcoming guests. In the center of the room, plenty of each kind of food is placed on a large, decorative copper tray, from which the guests serve themselves with a piece of bread. Hosts are never short of a seat, plate, or meal for an unexpected guest. This is how it must be, in this way of living, where hospitality is sacred.

The plaster wall that unifies space, by joining up the waviness of the ceiling beams, sometimes dips to create a storage recess, sometimes protrudes like a shelf, on which all those symbols of wealth and hospitality are kept: vases, aspergers, perfume-burners, and brass spittoons as shiny as gold.

Since hospitality is held in such high regard, its outward signs have to be ostentatious. On the shelves of the sheikh's *mafraj*, a host of vacuum flasks proclaims that all is ready to welcome as many guests as care to arrive. Thus are reputations established. Such is the obligation to offer hospitality, under threat of dishonor, that, when a member of the community refuses—after a dispute—to comply with the decisions made against him, the sheikh orders two men each day to invite themselves to the man's house. The wrongdoer must of course receive his imposed guests honorably and so, to avoid having gradually to sacrifice all his livestock, he quickly changes his mind.

In the al-Baydha region, beams set halfway up the wall, at the back of the room, hold a mountain of mattresses and blankets, which would not look amiss in a bedding store. Here, there is no hesitation as far as hospitality is concerned: nights are cold, distances long, occasions for celebrating frequent, and guests numerous. The hookah, its long pipe wrapped in bright colors, is passed round the guests, from mouth to mouth, and given pride of place in a specially designed recess cut in the thickness of the wall and underlined by a step frieze.

Similarly, the very firmament of the hut is filled with a huge collection of plates specially reserved for sumptuous banquets. Hung from the tent-top with ropes, the matting that is used as tablecloths and the large platters displayed await their cue to enter the scene. And to make the exhibition even more real, the painted murals show us the tea already served, pyramids of fruit tumbling from the tray, the hookah waiting to be smoked. The fizzy drinks in fresh colors make up for the lack of a refrigerator. The cone of the roof becomes a horn of plenty. The painted designs form a huge breadbasket overflowing with victuals.

At crossroads, shabby little restaurants invite you in, then turn into sumptuous palaces made of whitewashed brieze blocks, converted into art galleries. Everything is gold-framed: God's name, the proprietor's photo and operating license—with as many official stamps as you would find royal seals on a peace treaty—the Ma'rib dam and the Queen of Sheba's temple, the thoroughbred that almost won the American Cup, not forgetting the portrait of the President of the Republic, whose honored guest you have become for the duration of a meal.

The interior of a restaurant in Ma'rib, decorated with pictures and frames painted directly on the wall.

At Mohammad Burad Abdu's house in Qadamat Patash, the thermos of tea and the hookah are ready and waiting to celebrate the arrival in port of the fishermen's boat.

Chinese porcelain coffee cups and Duralex tea glasses await guests, set out on the decorated wall of Ali Mohammed's home at Dayr Heyran.

Platters, plates, bowls, and glasses are part of the interior decor of this hut at Dayr Heyran. The recesses set at bed height are ventilation inlets. The house is periodically refloored with an earth and dung mixture streaked into wave patterns.

Once the domestic chores and agricultural work are over, the
women meet in each others' houses every afternoon to puff on the
hookah and, sometimes, to dance or chew qat.

A collection of hookahs has pride of place next to the television set:
their presence in great numbers is the mark of a notable
household.

The table, kettle, teapot, thermos, and hookah are explicit enough, so that even illiterates have no need to read "Welcome to Salem Zawen's café-restaurant."

*Welcome to the home of Mohammad Chawki
Jubara, in the village of Qudamat Qubara,
northern Tihama.*

*The profusion of enamelled platters and plates are in
themselves a welcome, repeated in the inscription on
the painted frieze: "Happiness and good fortune to
all our guests each day."*

These spiralled baskets, sold in the
Sa'da souk and used as breadbaskets,
are made by women from the small
Jewish communities in the vicinity.

The roof of the hut is a constellation of starry lines
spangled with colors. From time to time, a bird,
attracted by the shady coolness and the decorative
branches, will come and perch on the rope hanging
from the ceiling.

At Bayt Ghanima, San'a, the place of honor or "head" in the reception room is surmounted by a calligraphy of Allah, a Koran in its brocade cover, a portrait of the head of the household, a certificate, and some souvenir plates brought back from Cairo by the son. Laid out on the shelves are all the utensils required for receiving guests: a vase, an asperger, and a coffeepot.

Bayt Ahmad Ghaleb, at ad-Dahi, boasts the most generous,
hospitable decor. The items chosen by the master of the house
reflect what has come on to the market most recently.
Machine-woven carpets with Turkmenian patterns,
machine-embroidered antimacassars from China, printed
tapestries, mirrors, garlands, spangled calligraphy, gold-edged
bowls, shiny metal goblets, and enamelled plates.

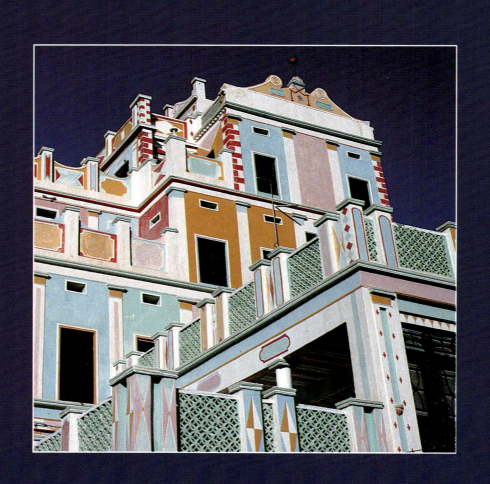

THE RAINBOW HOUSE

Beneath the sky's prism, the house picks out through
the rain all the colors of the sun. The light, now diffused
into brilliant hues, becomes a painting.

Photographed in 1995 at al-Munira, this decor was created in 1978 by Halima Ahmed Uthman, for the wedding of Yahya Ahmed Wald. Particularly noteworthy is one of the treasures making up the bride's dowry: a large necklace of heavy metal coins.

Pages 156–157: Painted doors in the Sa'da region.

PAINTING HAPPINESS

Wickerwork on the outside, clay on the inside, the huts of the Tihama are round or rectangular in shape. The work is shared, with the men building the structure while the women take care of the interior walls. These are coated with a mixture of clay and mud, enriched with chopped straw and dung, thrown on and smoothed out; whitewash may be applied on top of this. The overhanging elements of the structure, coated with a veil of clay, divide the area into compartments, creating pegs, hooks, shelves, and recesses. At points that are wisely chosen to capture the sea breezes, the lack of interior covering means that the home can be properly ventilated. This interior wall-coating is the foundation for decoration, carried out by the women themselves or by well-known specialists who are commissioned to do the work. In the village of al-Munira, the decoration has been done for a wedding. The young couple have come to spend their first night here, and the rest of their lives, beneath a sky painted the colors of happiness—a honeymoon and lucky stars marking out a path of tenderness and fertility.

Walls can talk. They speak to us in a language called desire. Do we have to know how to read and write in order to transform our familiar universe? If drawing is the first form of writing, then hieroglyphs are unnecessary, when all you need do to express your dreams is draw a colored line on a whitewashed wall. The shell in which we live then starts to look more festive, dresses up, lets itself go, and paints the world of our desires. The images work their magic and turn the surrounding desert into a shady garden. Then these dreams of greenery meet the desire for eternal abundance: coffeepots always full, fizzy drinks forever chilled, bunches of grapes ever ripe, hookahs waiting in the tobacco-rich cinders, and orange trees bending under the weight of their fruit.

The houses drawn are a thousand leagues from the local mud-huts: we see castles with towers and royal flags flying. The wickerwork of the roof is an aviary for parading, affronted peacocks that, from time to time, deign to spread their iridescent ocelli in the street. All these "eyes," and the rich colors, are real weapons in the continuous fight against the evil eye.

Here, dedicated to the mistress of the house, a gifted seamstress, sits the sewing machine, for the moment in its place of honor on the wall. But some day soon, God willing, it will come down into the middle of the room, materializing into real Chinese cast iron ornamented with golden dragons. To complete this idyllic picture of success and coming prosperity, the husband will soon make his fortune as a barber: clippers, scissors, and razors are already within reach. Heavy gold jewelry, bracelets, breastplates, and earrings are painted beside a series of dots, joining up to make endless pearl necklaces. The garlands of fruit and flowers weave crowns of happiness for the fortunate inhabitants. Beyond the explanations put forward and the supposedly harmless daydreams, the decoration nevertheless spreads out a whole world of desired opulence. To paint is to possess.

The language of decoration can also relate what Tradition tells us: the miracle of the spider's web, woven to hide the entrance to the cave where Mohammed hid from his pursuers; the Prophet's fantastic ride on his winged horse, Buraq, that carried him in one leap from Medina to Jerusalem; the glorious battles against the infidel; the great moments of Islam; the revered disciples, missionaries, and warriors.

As the stained glass panels in cathedrals relate the Good Book to the ignorant, these paintings are a support for religious instruction. Painted in each individual square of the wall, the drawing evolves like a comic strip.

The different stages of the pilgrimage are shown: the sea-crossing, Medina, Mecca, the stone-throwing against temptation by the devil at Mina, the water from Zemzem and the circumambulation of the Ka'ba.

Now the firmament of the mud-hut has become an artist's impression of Paradise.

Using a team of zebus, a level area is prepared for the construction of a new hut in the village of Qadamat Patash.

The scene is set: a three-domed mosque, above which flits an airplane, God's name in calligraphy, and a castle with two towers framed by two huge bouquets. Come and look around Suq al-Khamis, Wadi Mawr.

Here is the painter Bilal at work in the village of Dayr al-Hudaby, Wadi Mawr. He has been specially commissioned to decorate the hut and is paid by the day. The owner, of course, also provides the artist with food and lodging. Bilal wishes to paint only the happier memories of his stay in Saudi Arabia.

*The prehistoric hunter used to draw incantatory hunting scenes
on his cave wall with precision and conviction; here the facade
of the fisherman's house catches silver fish in the net of its decor.*

*The intertwined branches are carefully
secured to form the conical structure of the
hut roof at Halifaya, Wadi Mawr.*

164

Two well-known families of painters—
Abdalla Abukar Hassan and Omar
Qishra—decorated these rectangular hut
interiors, in the village of Ibn 'Abbas,
about twenty years ago. Nowadays, new
buildings are constructed in cement
brieze blocks, with flat roof-terraces
devoid of painted decoration.

Social success must come when heavy, agricultural chores are succeeded by images of new, desirable trades: dressmaker, hairdresser.

The decor, dated 1388 in the Hegira calendar, shows a transistor radio, which was the peak of modernity then—on that day in 1967 in the Christian calendar—before television came to Ibn 'Abbas.

A twin-engine plane, its wings open, has landed right on top of a hut at Jabal Milhan.

VISION OF A FUTURISTIC WORLD

The artist's brush is a magic wand that transforms the familiar donkey into a shining motorbike, with an added touch of common sense—the tools necessary to repair it in case of breakdown. The camel turns into a rocket, a jet, or a helicopter. The fine film of color supports a space for dreams where there are abundant harvests, as much as supersonic modernity.

At the very top of the hut, an airplane, a token of progress, has somehow managed gently to touch down and is now protecting the dwelling with its widespread wings. The choice of landing strip for these different aircraft proves they have a good eye for heights. The target given to the variable geometry jet-fighters is clear: aim between the eyes, between the windows. Mission accomplished, right on the bull's-eye: victorious beep-beeps fill the air. Deep inside symbolic strategic HQ, the airplane has linked up the inhabitants of the house with the forces of the cosmos.

The visionary artist transforms the hut into an apartment block with elevator. He "hitches his tank to a star" and, in spite of the sandstorm sweeping under the door, takes off toward the galaxy of progress. When he returns, he has become a heroic explorer who has seen the city with his own eyes; he picks out the seven colors of the rainbow, in the shape of restaurants, record-players, cassette-decks, steamers, fire-engines, and three-color traffic signals.

When the sailor who has sailed the seven seas comes home to his tiny village, set between dry salt piles and the ebb-tide's foam, everyone sees him as the harbinger of new discoveries and inventions.

After a lifetime's slaving in ships' holds, he does not talk about the deafening roar and infernal heat of the machines. He says nothing of this world which was his, with mingling dust and sweat, black grease and burning oil around the propeller shaft, the loneliness and toil. He forgets it all, as the gold prospector forgets all the exhausting panning for nothing but sand, recalling only the gleaming nuggets. On the wall, he draws a long, air-conditioned limousine sliding silently through the whitewashed night. It dazzles us, astounds us, this cavalcade under our noses, watched by the President of the Republic himself, as he stands proudly to attention on the national day, high on his official platform. The sailor paints fleeting images of ports-of-call, skyscrapers, and the constant flow of traffic, reflected in the mirror-walls of these strongholds of glass and wealth that are now his own.

A filter from an engine-housing, set in clay and haloed with color, is just as much an exhibit as a ventilation inlet in perfect working order. The transistor and the "picture box" come down from the wall right into the center of the room. San'a, Aden, the whole world can be picked up here. Big metal-weave ears blossom everywhere. At Ibn 'Abbas, a fishing village on the Red Sea, the satellite disk is too big for the top of the hut, so it has taken root in the brushwood hedge. On clear days, the driftnet of the image-catchers, off Djibouti, transmits as far as here blurred snatches of teleshopping from Paris, in the form of gray, moving lines. Now, in place of the unvoiced music of morse code, comes the singing of advertising sirens, long-distance.

City walls tumble into billboards. A passer-by's shadow turns into a cowboy with filter-tip cigarettes. Along the roadsides, strange trees have sprouted and, although their fruits are tempting, they are not always edible. Designed to be seen driving past at top speed, the billboards do not make much sense to the shepherd resting in the shade they provide.

The motorized world has spread over the entire country: generators, mills, and trucks have set up a network of noisy sound waves that continually spreads. The deafening bangs and backfires seem as much appreciated as the rifle-shots that celebrate all happy events. A made-to-measure, fitted cover very quickly protects a stationary vehicle and, so that it remains immobile, its overcoat deliberately matches the house's color scheme.

Western fashion is worn on the walls, painted life-size, on top-model figures. In the heat of Aden, it is better to leave the strangling necktie where it belongs—on the advertisements sketched on store shutters. Modernity has taken to generalized kidnapping of ancient customs.

The words airplane and bird have the same root in Arabic. The same motif graces the forehead of this Bedouin woman, from the village of Melaha, Wadi Majzar, as appears between the windows of this house.

The fascination for the new means of transportation is tempered by common sense and caution. The tool kit is drawn well in view, as though to ward off any possible breakdowns.

Every morning, on Taghrir Square, a butcher from the old city of San'a takes a taxi-motorbike with a sheep, which he slaughters by cutting its throat, at the El Ga city abattoir. A half hour later, he comes back by taxi-motorbike, then goes and butchers the carcass to sell the meat in his small store at Bab Saba.

In keeping with tradition, the truck-driver from Najran has had a camel painted on his cab door. It reminds him of the camel that he carefully keeps back at the camp, "just in case the prosperity brought by oil ever dries up," he says.

*Veiled beneath their made-to-measure covers, cut to fit
around the wing mirrors, the trucks wait patiently for their owners,
sheltered from dust and rain, on a platform set above the flood line of Wadi Yahar.*

*The stripes on the lower part of this building at Ralab, Jawf,
make it look even more solid, but stop at door level.*

Inside this egg-shaped hut is a building with an elevator rising to each floor—thus has the painter Ibrahim Bissayli designed his house at Ibn 'Abbas.

*On Kuwait Street, San'a, the store belonging to the satellite
disk installer shows previews of what consumers can expect.*

What outfit would you choose as most suitable for Aden's climate, which has high humidity and temperatures of forty degrees centigrade in the shade: white shirt and necktie, with slim-fitting trousers, and a tailored jacket, or futa, *open shirt, and turban? Beyond considerations of comfort, how we dress is a matter of culture.*

Advertisements for condensed or powdered milk have spread over the doors in San'a.

Highly colored pyramids of sweet delights spill over the front of the Crater patisserie in Aden.

CHROMATIC INVASION

W hite stone, black stone, empty squares, full squares: the checkerboard evenly divides up the area, alternating black and white, for maximum effect and contrast.

Color erupts, replaces the black and white, breaks up light into its component parts. Each square takes on a different shade, and a harlequin costume is born. This imaginative pattern, which quickly became synonymous with fun and witticisms, began life as an ascesis, or self-discipline. The Sufi mystics, in their spiritual search for God, have renounced tempting luxuries, and wear a simple, woolen garment, a *suf* (wool). The dervishes and other wandering monks, in their humility, dress only in scraps of fabric sewn together, in rags they have begged for. Thus there appeared these bits of nothing that cover the world with their beauty, from the Korean *pojaguis* to the patchworks of the Amish. The sole purpose of each fragment is to emphasize its neighbor, to set off the colors of surrounding pieces.

The meditation mats used by the Birman monks resemble fabric mats made by the women of Hadramawt—from plaited strips, frugally saved cloth leftovers, and knotted ribbons—fabric works of art, in fact, that could be exhibited next to those signed "Pollock."

Those whom the Earth, in her limited generosity, could not feed went off in search of adventure across the sea. They have come back with their heads and their arms full of colors from faraway places, carrying visions of other worlds, made richer by so much trade. The holds of the color-splashed boats overflow with different-colored merchandise: spices from plantations, gems of manufacturing, and shiny new mechanical wonders. The color of the ship itself is contagious. The protective pigments that coat the wood of the dhows are also used enthusiastically on doors and windows, which must also fend off insect attacks and the ravages of the weather. Paint-pot leftovers are spread over landbound vessels.

Everything happens as though, on their arrival from the industrialized world, machines and appliances had to pass through a customs process of emotional adoption, not being allowed in unless first splashed with color. This is how modernity is tamed. The brand-new four-wheel drive vehicle sees its hood and radiator grille transformed into a familiar muzzle, with two languorous eyes; the bumper is doubly protected with flowers better to avoid, or absorb, any unexpected encounters. The vehicle's interior becomes a reception room with cushions, carpets, tapestries on the ceiling, pictures of Eastern stars with love-struck, doe's eyes and buxom decolletés, beneath the plastic frame. A new jewel for men—token of its master's fortune wherever he goes—is the car-key, laced around with attractive bands, trimmed with bright beads, and worn crossed-over round the *janbiya*.

The transistor radio is dressed up in a *futa* of braiding and tassels, chosen with the utmost care, so that it exactly matches the color scheme of its owner's clothing. The box of paper tissues, like the gas pump, is enshrined in a multicolored tabernacle. The fat Normandy cow, proudly displayed on concentrated milk, with her generous udders, black and white markings, comes and grazes on arid doors. She lets her calves run riot in the souks, performing acrobatic feats with no safety net, balancing in daring pyramids on shaky shelves.

Everywhere there is movement and change. Being able to transport stones from distant quarries, by truck, to the construction site has made polychromy possible. The capital's wealthiest home-owners compete in their demands for deliveries of stones: they no longer order only limestone-white and basalt-black, but also blocks that are pistachio-green, pigeon-blood red, and candy-pink. Color seems to have exploded into a firework display: gates, walls, headdresses, veils, beads, TVs, nothing escapes.

The chromatic invasion is gaining ground everywhere, invading and sweeping away all in its path. No one is safe and, therefore, no one should be surprised, one of these days, to wake up grating their teeth at the craziest, most intense colors ever put together by a master pastrycook. Houses metamorphose into melting candies. Flavorful colors spice up everyday gray.

Coloring our world turns out to be one of the major art forms: it is purely and simply an *art de vivre*.

Decked out in its colored finery, the new steed silently boasts its owner's pride.

Color is gaining ground everywhere and has even taken the place of black and white. Thus, the nine-story mud palace of the Buqshan family, in the village of Geylah, Wadi Daw'an, is a thousand leagues from the white network drawn on this facade in the village of Helf, Jabal Gheylan. The black and white stone checkerboard set between the lintel and the relieving arch, at az-Zahari near al-Baydha, becomes polychrome at Bani Baqr.

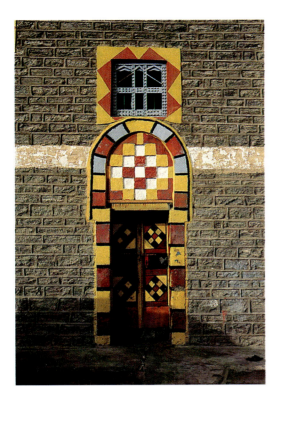

The bright paint that protects the hulls of the wooden dhows has now spread to the metal doors, signed by the Ibn Hageb workshop.

After being waterproofed in the port of al-Hudayda, the dhows sail away again, plowing the Red Sea and Indian Ocean.
The old wooden vessels, stitched with ropes, are no longer built today.

Page 182: Mud palace in the village of Khugekher, Wadi Daw'an.
Page 183: *The painting in this house in Wadi Daw'an, belonging to the Buqshan family, is the work of Abu Hussein of Tarim.*

At Harib, most paint is usually applied to the wooden shutters and
the window surrounds.

In the village of Rijaya, near at-Turba, the texture of the chipped
stones inspires a spontaneous overflow of color.

*Open to the ocean breezes, here is the store of Mr Abdalla Ali and son,
in 6 June District, al-Qishn.*

*The geometry of the support used in no way limits the colorists' creative
freedom: checkerboards in Wadi Bana, lines and surfaces at Utma,
diamonds at al-Juma and in the souk at al-Madraq.*

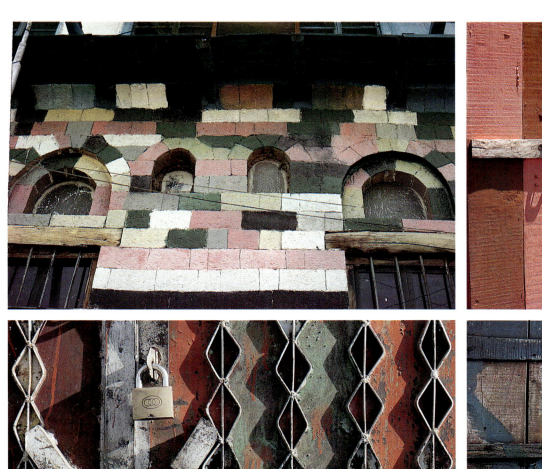

Radio-cassette player carefully decked out in its owner's colors at as-Sawadiya.

Entrance porch, in the village of Sif, in the Wadi Daw'an. The disguised door has a small central opening which allows the visitor to be identified.

Reception room in the Bayt Buqshan, known as diwan or the "mother of four" in reference to the four pillars that compose it. Doors set between the wall panels create storage space for blankets and quilted bedspreads.

*Amidst strip light candelabras, the gas pumps are set on a pedestal,
erect in their metal casings, which are painted in flat tints then
brightened up with lighter brush strokes.*

A store in the al-Juma souk. The blue of the clothing and the green color of qat *when chewed seem, along with yellow, to be the store owner's favorite colors.*

At Utma, on this Suq Salous door, the calligraphy reads: "Crescent Moon Workshop of Mohammed Ali, artist and owner."

"In the name of God, the merciful, the bountiful. All this has been accomplished by the grace of God," reads the inscription on this facade between Huth and al-Qabai.

*In the Wadi Zabab souk, the Tyrian pink turban extends the
dazzling smile of this lady trader.*

*A carpet made from knotted cloth strips, in the palace
of Abbas al-Kaf, Tarim.*

Photography by Pascal and Maria Maréchaux, 19 rue Deparcieux, 75014 Paris
Text by Pascal Maréchaux
Design by Pascal Maréchaux
Typesetting by Octavo Editions
Origination: Evolutif A.G., Montrouge

Translated from the French by Kathleen Guillaume
Edited by Kate Swainson

Flammarion
26 rue Racine
75006 Paris

200 Park Avenue South, Suite 1406
New York
NY 10003

Published simultaneously in French under the title *Tableaux du Yémen* © Les Éditions Arthaud, Paris, 1997.

ISBN: 2-08013-647-X

Numéro d'édition: FA3647-02
Dépôt légal: September 1997
Printed and bound by G. Canale & Co. SpA, Borgaro Torinese

Printed in Italy

Library of Congress Cataloging-in-Publication Data

Maréchaux, Pascal.
        [Tableaux du Yémen.   English]
        Impressions of Yemen / Pascal and Maria Maréchaux; [translated
    from the French by Kathleen Guillaume].
            p.   cm.
        Includes bibliographical references.
        ISBN 2–08–013647–X
        1. Yemen—Pictorial works.   I. Maréchaux, Maria.   II. Title.
    DS247.06M3713   1997   97–27817
    953.3—dc21